BEING IN BETWEEN

BEING IN BETWEEN

POEMS BY
Yolanda Koumidou

Produced by Yolanda Koumidou © 2019

Front cover sunset photograph: Yolanda Koumidou © 2017

Cover design: Marietta Anastassatos
Inside design: Keith Sheridan

Website: www.veiledsoul.com

Contact: ykoumidou@gmail.com

ISBN: 978-1-5323-9440-9

Other Poetry Collections
by
Yolanda Koumidou

B O O K S
in English
Merciless Path
Veiled Soul (CD)

B O O K S
in Greek
Kypros 1974 (Cyprus 1974)
Kimmatisti mou Zoe (My Wavy Life)
Poems of Yolanda Koumidou-Vlesmas

For my mother Keti and my father Nico

TABLE OF CONTENTS*

Inner Explorations

EVOLVING LOVE

FLOWING INSPIRATION

Personal Dedications

*Location: Most poems were written in Lynbrook NY, unless otherwise stated.

ACCUMULATED WISDOM

THE BLOCKS

thought
they were blocks
blocking the Path

realized
they ARE the Path

ATTEMPTING EMPTINESS

never before
fullness was noticed
until emptiness was attempted

BACKBITING

tongue's poisoned arrows
never reach their intended target

like boomerangs
they return
releasing their poison
straight into the archer's heart

THE DEATH OF A PERFECT MOMENT

Woombye, Australia

there is never a time
when mourning is so palpable as
while living a "perfect moment"
desiring to
grasp it
have it repeat itself
make it last

and failing

THE INNER FIRE

keeping the fire burning
the Zoroastrian priests
five times a day
feed the fire
for thousands of years
feeding the fire
the flame kept alive

how to keep the Inner Fire burning?
how to feed it?
with what?
no "priests" are coming

with bare hands
with bloody fingers, if you have to,
chisel time and space in life's details
unearth the Wood Sticks
feed the Fire
keep it burning
keep alive...

THE ARRIVAL

Assisi, Italy

arriving at inner peace:
*   receiving what was not wanted*
*   with no disappointment*
*   getting what was desired*
*   with no excitement*
*   waiting for nothing*
*   accepting what comes*
for sure
many a storm must have preceded this kind of Arrival

WHAT IS RECEIVED

never know what is needed
finding out only through
what is received

THE SOUL REVEALED

if only we were able
to break through from our daily Fog!
we will be blinded
by "Our" brilliance...

MEETING THE ARTIST

a masterpiece
is different from its creator

when art reaches you
it is just that

do not confuse it
to be equal to its creator
developing a desire in meeting him

the artwork was created in a rare moment
when
attachments of any kind were released
when
the artist was unlike herself

soon after
he came back to his "senses"
becoming just like you

no need in getting to know her
because
you already do

IN THE DESSERT

entering the Dessert
vastness, emptiness
nothingness it seems at first

yet this is where Thirst is born

do not quench it
through Mirages again
search for the Source

It
has been waiting for you...

TRAVERSING

arriving and departing
from others' life
and they from ours

moving on
hopefully with less
not more

UNTITLED

Myrtle Beach, South Carolina
(woke up with these words in my mouth)

*an unexamined life
is a life
waiting to be repeated*

ROCKS AND THOUGHTS

when the heart
gets filled with thoughts
is like a river
getting filled with rocks
obstructing the Flow

TUG-OF-WAR

God takes something away from everyone
and everyone
wants that something back

one can spend a life time
in this tug-of-war

and one does

THE OTHER SIDE OF "VICES"

thank you
blessed sensation of disappointment
invaluable reminder
every time the "wants" override
intuition's dictation

thank you
blessed sensation of anger
precious teacher
pointing out when desires get interrupted
diverting ego's prepared plan

thank you
blessed sensation of jealousy
highlighting the grip of
the "mine" and "being better than" states

thank you
blessed sensation of worry
loyal companion
revealing the ever present lack of trust
in God's Will

thank you
blessed sensation of judgment
bringing forth
that which awaits integration

without your constant reminders
the knock of awakening
would have not been heard

THE TIME BETWEEN

how is life when
inhales and exhales
are barely distinguishable

that's how life is
when a poet
doesn't write
languishing and flourishing
barely distinguishable

MIGHTY SANSKARAS*

*Sanskaras: Accumulated mental impressions of the history of our animal and human existences which tend to superimpose themselves on our present impressions. (for more detailed description read *Discourses* by Meher Baba).

LIKE SPIDERS

like spiders
day and night
with every thought, word and action
we weave new Cobwebs

unlike spiders
we
get caught in them

SANSKARIC MIGHT

Carmel, NY

the sheer force
of water
hidden in a drop

the mighty power
of wind
lurking inside the breeze

the utter might
of sanskaras
folded in thoughts
once unfolded
you might as well try to stop
tidal waves and tornados

RESURRECTION

and when you were certain
one of your sanskaras
was put to rest
one day
it resurrects itself
it is alive again
as if
all the efforts shedding it
having it removed
never took place

what a brilliant act
of playing dead!

Happy New Year

not to worry
only the year will change tonight

your sanskaras
remain faithfully steady
waiting for you in the morning

POT HOLES

sanskaras
must be round in shape
like the wheel
rolling on and on
uninterrupted repetition

except
when wheel meets pot hole
a chance to break
to come apart
to repeat no more

welcoming
life's Pot Holes
the only way out!

THE HEWING

this piece of Wood
needs hewing

to be cut off from its history
the mother tree
from the ways it thinks it should be

to surrender
to the blows of its Sculptor
willing to become unrecognizable
letting the Sculptor hew
the original figure
out of its current form....

DESTRUCTIONS

seeking out
the Creator of Beauty

but getting stuck
on creation's beauty, instead

SANSKARA DEPARTING

Sydney, Australia

the warmth of the Flesh
gone
the circulating Blood
the pulsating beating of the Heart
all gone
only its Skeleton remaining now
marching in the usual stride
but lifeless

on the road to extinction

FAMILIARITY

Familiarity
predictable repetition
feeding sanskaras
curtailing intuition
yet,
popular among the many

the Unfamiliar
familiar
only to a few, if any

INNER EXPLORATIONS

ABANDON SEARCH

for years
searching for a companion
to walk the Path together

alas
only one set of footprints
fit on this Path

abandon search

BREATHING THE MOMENT

breathing in, the moment
devoid of expectations
half a lifetime of breaths had to be taken
before arriving to
breathing in, the moment

Zip Lining

Dominical, Costa Rica

trusting is like
zip lining backwards

sliding fast
that thin cable
without seeing where you go
not knowing
if someone will catch you
while bestowed with fear
it carries an unexpected thrill

when you crashed
on life's Cable
you bruised
filled with fear
you stopped riding the line
time to get back on that Cable
for the unexpected thrill of trusting

THE RIM OF THE ABYSS

standing at the Rim
the Leap, not taken yet

tethered to the pole of comfort
held down by the fetters of image
anchored to the need for approval

at least the path was found
and the Rim is reached

SOAKED IN THE MOMENT

open heart
devoid of
waiting
expecting
wanting

not too much experience yet
in being soaked in the moment

IGNORANT HANDS

one by one
the Knots are untied
with my own two Hands

they were always free
but ignorant to their divine inherent Talent

ACCEPTANCE

going to take a walk
enter the doors which are open
knock on closed ones
and walk passed the ones remaining locked

Autumn

Schoharie, NY

autumn
time for release
and the leaves surrender

why can't i
let go like them
why the delay
the unnecessary holding on
the resistance to the arrival
of life's Autumns

TIME TO GO

it has been said, time doesn't exist
i beg to differ, having evidence in flesh and bone to prove it

stretching occurred in places admired for their firmness
changes in color occurred without even spending a dime on hair color
changes in height and weight occurred just like wet clothes,
   shrinking and becoming heavier

walking down the street invisible

how terrible
yet
how liberating

since flesh and bones don't do it anymore
arrived at the Time to Go inwards...

diving in the depths of a new Dwelling
and to a shocking amazement, discovering the place where,
time,
actually, does not exit

there has been a gain, not loss, in strength and beauty
nothing was touched here, since eons of time

most certainly, Time to Go

Moving On

going backwards
because do not know
where else to go

how to move on
how to think new thoughts
how to give new responses

patterns
repeating

patterns
with predictable existence

how does one
become unpredictable
to one's self?

how does one
move on?

EXPECTING NOTHING

love dawning
in a new Light
without expecting anything
not even to be received

EVOLVING DURING ONE'S "ABSENCE"

left
went Away for a long time
often this happens
like it or not

upon my return
a new self was awaiting
a new self met me at the door
what a surprise

don't have to be present
for the present to evolve

BIRTH DAYS

sometimes
remaining Pregnant for days, weeks, months,
years even

full of unexpressed life
it gets painful, i tell you

then one day
multiple Births

can't fathom the pain
the Pregnant ones never giving Birth suffer

cannot

So Far...

glimpses of the Soul
not found in bright white lights
not even in peacefulness
or blissful moments
so far...anyway

glimpses of the Soul
in the bowels of darkness
in the abyss of loneliness
so far...anyway

AREAS OF EXPERTISE

Myrtle Beach, South Carolina

excellent skills in judging
ability to immediately classify anyone as
good or bad
beautiful or ugly
right or wrong

impressive skills in craving
rare ability to maintain a state
of constant wanting or not wanting
additional skills include
the ability to suffer and worry at the drop of a hat

guarantee to activate and utilize these skills
anywhere
at any time

NO THING

used to
hold on to anticipatings
excitements
and falling in many loves

used to
hold on to worries
disappointments
and drowning in deep pains

all that uprooted now
shallow were their roots

no thing to hold on to anymore
no hope

no thing

YOUR DAAMAN

when romance descends
i forget You
when pain invades
when anger prevails
i forget You
when excitement comes
i forget You

and remember
only me.

A Working Poet (but not as a poet)

this time
side Streets
became the Main Road
and the Main Road
the Side Streets

WHERE I LIVE

time to live
where i am

WHERE IS IT

Montauk, NY

at what point
did i lose
that obedience
which carries no complain
that surrender
which accepts what comes
the kind the trees and oceans carry

or has it been there, dormant in my existence
waiting
for me to claim
what has always been mine
but got lost in the shuffle of desires

NATURE

Montauk, NY

nature
doing what it needs to do
based on the season

doing what i want to do
based on my desires

well,
this is
my
nature

or is it?

NEW CAST

these new thoughts and feelings
not fitting the old Mould

suspended
until fresh Cast is cut

suffering in the meantime

STUCK IN THE MOMENT

once anticipation and reminiscing
are under control
one gets stuck
in the moment

EVOLVING LOVE

LOOSING

have loved
and gained

gained awareness
of what i need to lose

PREREQUISITE TORTURE

how to tolerate
the lack
of gentle stroking
of skins touching

how to tolerate
not falling in love

is this a prerequisite torture
before the longing
recalculates its route towards the Destination

BIRTHING THE ENDING

the ending stirred inside
like a fetus longing for birth
the Ninth Month arrived

after years

FOOD FOR THE SOUL

gaze at beauty
go love someone
feed the soul

ROMANCE

a night dream
cannot be ordered to appear
the visits, spontaneous
the content, unpredictable
it descends
offers all it has to offer
then departs
lingering
is not its nature

identical
to romance course

ROMANTIC LOVE POEMS

written colorful words
painting images of Love
passion emanating through them
but limited by the Ceiling
of human love

written profound language
but
depth is penetrating the words
not
the Depth

OBSESSION MY LOVE

peripheral vision disappears
the agony of wanting takes over
thoughts
get stuck like the needle on a record
life narrows down
to a trickling stream of misery

confusing it with loving
how bizarre
the only loving happening here
is loving to be obsessed

obsession my love
time to peal you off

RESTRAINT NOT NEEDED

missed
the myriad opportunities
to use retraint
nothing to restrain now
the passions
have been tamed
credit does not belong here
do not know whom it belongs to

but i can take a guess...

TURNING TO DUST

...then the loves
all dried up
cracking, crumbling
turning to Dust

dust resting on the heart
when would the wind blow?

LOVING

it took being in love
to remove the thorn of "falling in love"
the most severe obstacle
to Loving

THE VIEWING

broken to pieces again
nature and history teach:
when put back together
new the combination will be
different the revealed image

anticipating the viewing

is the only comfort
holding together
this heart right now

LOVE AND HOME

Love is Home
Home is Love

FLOWING INSPIRATION

BEING IN BETWEEN

on the move
from lower to higher desires
in the mean time...

being in between

dreaming
what is well known to be just a dream
longing
what is well known to be a transient destination
this being in between
this migration
holds sights not yet seen
holds only given promise

at least there was a move
at least i departed!

A Birth

pen to paper
a poem awaits its birth

THE JUNGLE

Dominical, Costa Rica

the green of the jungle
you think you enter it
but it enters you

it activates the mouth to shut
the spirit to speak
and the hand to write...

ONE WAY CONVERSATION

Dominical, Costa Rica

night time
in the Costa Rican jungle
nothing much to say
what do you talk about
when all life,
other than human,
synchronizes
in a symphony under the stars
you stop and listen
responding in silence
or not at all

perfect time
for one way conversation

THOSE MORNINGS

Ojai, California

and then
there are those mornings
arriving with so much beauty
you do not know what to do with it
how to hold it
how to capture it
you close your eyes
and let the pores of your being inhale it

the spirit is fed
for today

THE FIRST LIGHT OF THE DAY

being present each morning
to the sun's first light

letting it awake the spirit
to the unpredictability
folded inside the new day

Under Baba's Tree

Ojai, California (January, 2016)

a giant of a tree
half burned
survivor trunk
branches like whole bodies
wrapped in dry, cracked skin
bowing down, all around

masculine and feminine
entangling
the enormous, powerful, thick branches
holding
the fluttering, small, tender leaves

birds
sing a short song
then move on
yellow leaves
finishing this life time
carpeting the tree floor
offering last service
before decaying

a sweet aroma, not knowing where from
penetrating the air
sun sneaking through any possible opening
between the green leaves
holding strong
with life still to live

a remarkable Silence
encasing all these sounds and sights
when it descends
nothing is needed
nothing else is remotely necessary

yet the mind
still succeeds in its invasions
about what to do next, when and how
but the Silence, this Silence
like blanket over fire
quickly covers and extinguishes
mind's futile meanderings

the Silence, prevailing
this Silence
His Silence

∞

PERSONAL DEDICATIONS

MY SON

For Erico

your presence
identical to the instrument you play
bass
the power immense
rarely front stage
yet holding and carrying the Band

your compassion and kindness
omnipresent

your temper, when necessary
scorching fire

your determination
fierce and sharp as a machete
clearing whatever stands in your way

your depth
silent, unseen
visible and palpable
only to those who have been there

your smile
melting any heart
no matter its state

your eye
an eagle's eye
no possible escape

my son
the road wide open in front of you
traverse well
armed with who you are

THE EMPTY BED

Coffs Harbor, Australia

For a friend's mother

and he said
lets go to the hospital
we did
the bed was empty
an abyss opened
nobody noticed me falling in it
it was a silent drop
into a depth from where
no young heart ever recovers

My Mother Keti

For my mother

slender
green eyes
bright permanent smile
a heart ignorant of hate
so what if
at the end she got her thoughts scrambled
so what if
she confused her words
she spoke through actions
actions which never refused
offering, doing, gifting
generously
always
actions which spread giving
quietly

a true saint living at home in Lynbrook, New York
performing daily domestic miracles
my mother
who lived a depended life
who could not give advice
who did not philosophize
who did not speak English
who did not know how to be there in difficult times
but
gave "mothering" a new meaning
not written in cards
my mother
wrote her own card with
non-ending, spontaneous, innocent, selfless, flowing, authentic, heartfelt
LOVING

MY FRIEND LISTENING TO ME

For Renate

you take what i say
take in your hands
its fragility recognized

and you dance
a soft, dervish dance
the words' petals falling off
revealing
that which lies closer to the Core

through your listening
i hear
the Word which my words cloud

Farewell to Meher Mount

Ojai, California (January, 2017)

For Meher Mount

the days
caretaking paradise
are now coming to a close

how to say farewell
to Meher Mount

to the silent rises and settings
of the sun's yellows and pink and mauves
to the wet drumming of the rains
the fog's layered veils
to the humming of the birds
the deer's persistent stare
and the casual stride of the coyote
to the blue mountains
to the green of the grass

how to say farewell
to His Presence
pulsating in stillness under His tree

how to say farewell
when one has
fared well on Meher Mount

one simply doesn't...

MY FATHER'S DEATH

For my father

The news arrived:
your soul was released

after the primal cry
after the hundreds of prayers
after the sharing of stories
the condolences, the burial
after the final salute
an unfamiliar sadness descended
penetrating the bones
and there it remained for months

the deep silence of death
echoes in the heart
the last image
beaming serenity
through that small window of the coffin
such calmness
accompanied your exit
satisfaction
for a life well lived for yourself

the news arrived
your soul is released

THE COMMONERS ARE FOOLED

Woombye, Australia

For A. C.

king in your castle
sitting on your throne
on top of the hill
above everyone else
in front of panoramic views
controlling
correcting
directing
with "kindness" and humor
secure coverings
for ignorance, lust and judgment lurking underneath

all commoners are fooled
since the castle appears as a hut
the throne as a stool
the royal attire as work clothes

all are being fooled
except this writer!

CURTAILED LIFE FORCE

For my friend the "monk monkey"

unexpressed touch

as if the sun
found no planet
to offer its light

as if color
could not be spread

as if music notes
were never played
and poems
remained un recited

as if inhales
did not turn to exhales

unexpressed touch
curtailed life force

YOUR HEART

For R.S., a war veteran

your heart
heard
saw
received
and gave
lots she didn't like

your heart
broke
bled
closed
and cried
from lots done to her

your heart
disapproved deeply
of some actions
you were forced to commit
you told me
between the lines
i heard

so,
understood
is the reason
for the double fencing
around her

understood
is the need
for the armed protection

understood
is her difficulty
in trusting

but,
understood
is also
her longing to be touched and held
you told me
between the lines
i heard

∞